D0856668

EARLY RENAISSANCE RELIEFS

EARLY RENAISSANCE RELIEFS

Essays by

Charles Avery, Andrew Butterfield

and Ulrich Middeldorf

Salander-O'Reilly Galleries

NEW YORK

This catalogue accompanies an exhibition from
January 9 to February 3, 2001

Salander-O'Reilly Galleries, LLC
20 East 79 Street New York, NY 10021
Tel (212) 879-6606 Fax (212) 744-0655
www.salander.com
Gallery hours: Monday–Saturday 9:30 to 5:30

TABLE OF CONTENTS

The inspiration to do a show dedicated to early Renaissance reliefs came to us a relatively short time ago, and it would have been impossible to mount this exhibition without the enthusiasm and generosity of the several private collectors who have graciously lent their works to the show. We are deeply greatful for their help.

Special thanks are also due to Prof.ssa Paola Barocchi and to S.P.E.S. Editrice, Florence for permission to reprint Prof. Ulrich Middeldorf's essay "Some Florentine Painted Madonna Reliefs." For comments, criticisms and help with photographs we are grateful to: Charles Avery, Everett Fahy, Giancarlo Gentilini, Laurence Kanter, Jack Soultanian and Margaret Schwartz.

The bibliographies in the enries are comprehensive, but not exhaustive.

Introduction

This exhibition features nine masterpieces of early Renaissance relief sculpture. Although relatively limited in number, the works on view nevertheless illustrate the key development of the genre in the period, namely, the dramatic expansion of the *pictorial* range of sculpture. Through the use of color, perspective, *rilievo schiacciato*, and other means, artists made sculpture the cognate and analog of painting, equally capable in the naturalistic description of the human form. This advance is apparent even in the first works of the Renaissance, the competition panels by Ghiberti and Brunelleschi of 1401–2, and it is a fundamental leitmotif throughout the art of the epoch. In the words of Vasari, "Sculpture and painting are truly sister arts, born of the same father, *disegno*, at the same time, in the same birth; one art does not proceed or follow the other." This relationship is exemplified by the works on view: the Benedetto da Maino models, made for the Annunciation altar in Naples, one of the high-points of pictorial sculpture of the Quattrocento; the Antonello Gagini relief, with its beautiful passage of *rilievo schiacciato*; the Madonna reliefs which aspire to unite the virtues of painting and sculpture.

The works gathered here illustrate nearly the full range of sculpture media in the Renaissance—marble, stucco, terracotta, cartapesta; only metal and terracruda are not represented. The eight works indicate as well a broad spectrum of functions and types of Renaissance relief, from bozzetto to finished marble, from altarpiece to private devotional image.

A special emphasis of the exhibition is the Madonna and Child relief in painted stucco and cartapesta. These reliefs were immensely popular in Quattrocento Florence; nearly every home had one, and many had several. Their popularity stemmed directly from a fervent desire for a tangible and direct relationship with god. Contemporary religious and pastoral texts stimulated and encouraged this desire. For example, the *Regola del governo di cura famigliare*, a popular handbook written in 1403 by the eminent Florentine reformer, Fra Giovanni Dominici, advised that one decorate the home with paintings and sculptures of "the Madonna with the Child in her arms, holding a little bird or a pomegranate. Good also are images of Jesus nursing, or asleep in the lap of the Madonna." Another influential manual, Pseudo-Bonaventura's *Meditations on the Life of Christ*, even instructed the reader to imagine what it would be like to: "Pick Hm up and hold Him in your arms. Gaze on His face with devotion and reverently kiss Him and delight in Him. Then return Him to the mother and watch her attentively as she cares for Him assiduously and wisely." The combination of painting and sculpture greatly increased an image's verisimilitude, and hence, its potential for magical and religious power.

Modern scholars have often assumed that painted stucco reliefs were of secondary importance, and they have routinely categorized them as "after" or "workshop." This is a modern prejudice, due to modern preconceptions about the hierarchy of media and the proper separation of sculpture and painting. In fact, Renaissance documents consistently indicate that stucco reliefs were highly valued autograph works of art, whose combination of painting and sculpture greatly added to their appeal. For example, in his *Ricordanze*, the Florentine painter Neri di Bicci refers to stucco reliefs of the Madonna and Child "by the hand" of Desiderio di Settignano ("di mano di Desiderio"); he uses exactly the same language as when he refers to an autograph marble by the artist. In 1462 Francesco Sforza, the ruler of Milan, ordered his ambassador in Florence to acquire two stucco reliefs of the Madonna "per mano de magistero Desyderio;" and the ambassador dealt directly with the artist himself about the acquisition. Furthermore, the price Sforza was willing to pay, 25 ducats for the pair, was substantial. It is about half the price that Desiderio paid for his house (60 ducats), and higher than the valuation of many of the paintings and objects recorded in the 1492 inventory of Lorenzo de' Medici's collection, where, for example, Piero della Francesca's portrait of the Duke of Urbino and Botticelli's Pallas Athena were each valued at 10 ducats, and Mino da Fiesole's marble portrait of Piero de' Medici was valued at 12 ducats. Obviously, Sforza would not have offered so much for anything less than an autograph work.

Beginning in the Neo-classical period critics and theorists decreed that sculpture should be achromatic. This led to a profound misunderstanding of the statuary of the past, and what is far worse, to the systematic overcleaning and stripping of hundreds and perhaps thousands of Renaissance works of art. During the last fifty years, attitudes about sculpture have changed once more; and artists have again begun to make works that blend the sculptural and the pictorial. A re-examination of Renaissance pictorial and polychrome sculpture is overdue.

Andrew Butterfield

The Relief in Renaissance Florence: An Overview

Charles Avery

The relief underwent a greater change in the early Renaissance in Florence than any other form of sculpture, indeed it was the first vehicle for the emergence of the new style. In the Middle Ages stylized renderings of scenes had satisfied people, often with figures of irrationally different scales and in incongruously disjointed settings that manifested little apprehension of real appearances. Now, a renewed examination with unprejudiced eyes of ancient Roman reliefs (whose pagan subjects had been reprehensible from a Christian point of view) which were to be seen on altars, sarcophagi, triumphal arches and columns suggested ways of enhancing a sense of realism and hence of drama. To this was added around 1420 an awareness of the scientific principles underlying the diminution of forms as they are further from the eye, which enabled artists such as Brunelleschi, Donatello, Masaccio and Alberti to produce convincing simulacra of real appearances. This was enhanced by a study of the way forms are modelled by light and shade. ¶ The trial reliefs, showing the *Sacrifice of Isaac*, that were made for the competition in 1401 over the executant of new bronze doors for the Florence Baptistry by Ghiberti and Brunelleschi were imbued with some of these characteristics. Ghiberti won, and although he was obliged to perpetuate the Gothic style of Andrea Pisano's doors by using the same, antiquated, quatrefoil frames, his long sequence of reliefs, while always retaining Gothic elements, shows increasingly a careful adoption and integration of unashamedly antique motifs. ¶ Ghiberti designed his narratives with a sure sense of visual drama, judiciously introducing borrowings from ancient sculpture, (e.g. the *Borghese Sarcophagus*, for the heads which project, like door-knobs, from the junctures of the frames). Ghiberti also included amidst the foliage round the frames vignettes of small creatures copied from nature: it is arguable whether they are a continuance of that trait of realism that enlivened Gothic art, or an innovation, typical of the Renaissance, in the quasi-scientific observation of nature. ¶ This initial set of doors took a quarter of a century to perfect, and, such was their success, that they

were immediately followed by a commission for another set, which occupied Ghiberti for another quarter of a century, in fact until the end of his career (unveiled 1452; Ghiberti died 1455). Here he was permitted to dispense with the old-fashioned and constricting scheme of ornamental frames, and so was able to expand his narratives from the Old Testament over ten large, rectangular panels. This enabled Ghiberti to vie with painting, in the inclusion of landscapes or architectural settings, just as Donatello was beginning to in the same decade. Michelangelo subsequently called the new doors with justification '*The Gates of Paradise*'. ¶ Ghiberti avoided excesses of violence or drama, such as inspired Donatello to some of his greatest, and most daring, masterpieces of relief sculpture. Donatello rapidly broke away from the stylistic education implanted by Ghiberti while he was apprenticed to him, and (influenced by his study of ancient Roman remains with Brunelleschi) soon evolved a personal style. This he expressed in very low-relief (*rilievo schiacciato*), a technique invented between about 1415 and 1425. Donatello effectively drew on the surface of a slab of marble with a pointed chisel, indicating pictorial depth by the use of linear and aerial perspective, rather than by physically excavating the marble. This innovative form of relief is so pictorial, that it drew him close in approach to Masaccio. In the most exemplary of such reliefs, the *Feast of Herod* (Musée des Beaux-Arts, Lille), Donatello adhered to the principles enunciated by Alberti in his *Treatise on Painting*, which must have been in preparation during the 1420s, even though it was published only in 1436. A rationally constructed space is defined by the straight lines of architecture, and then peopled with *dramatis personae* of varying size, according to their positions, but with their heads remaining on the same line (the principle of isocephaly). The same ideas were applied by Masaccio in his fescoes in the Brancacci Chapel (Church of the Carmine, Florence), while another of Donatello's reliefs, *The Ascension of Christ and the Giving of the Keys to St. Peter* (Victoria & Albert Museum, London), is like a miniature version of one of Masaccio's magisterial fresco, *The Tribute Money*. ¶ However, Donatello's sometime partner Michelozzo and their contemporaries Nanni di Banco and Luca della Robbia, all preferred to remain within the ancient Roman convention of high relief, which is easier to control in the carving, and more legible from a distance. The only sculptor who emulated the technique of *rilievo schiacciato* was Desiderio da Settignano and then only in a few reliefs. Desiderio never used bronze to replicate the effect of frenzied modelling in the original wax models for his reliefs, as Donatello had. ¶ The only other sculptor to try the technique and then only once, by way of a deliberate youthful experiment, was Michelangelo, in his *Madonna della Scala* (Casa Buonarotti, Florence). This was indebted to a similar, though smaller, marble panel normally attributed to Desiderio, called *The Dudley Madonna* (Victoria & Albert Museum, London). Michelangelo managed to make the subtle modelling of drapery look very much like the wax that he must have used to make his working model on a wooden panel. He evidently rejected this approach thereafter, as being inappropriate for sculpture, inasmuch as painting provided a better means of rendering such scenes and achieving such subtlety of effect. He did carve a *Battle of Lapiths and Centaurs* in marble in the classical technique of relief (Casa Buonarotti, Florence), cutting much more deeply into the marble and thus relieving his figures almost to their full depth. Even this seems not to have pleased him, as is perhaps indicated by the fact that he left the panel unfinished (the first of many such relics of abandoned projects) but he kept both panels for the rest of his life, perhaps as evidence of his youthful prowess, or as an object lesson for himself and others of the deficiencies, as he saw them, of relief-carving as a branch of sculpture. He used the technique only twice more, relatively early in his maturity, for representations of the Virgin and Child in roundels of marble (*Pitti Tondo*, Museo Nazionale del Bargello, Florence; *Taddei Tondo*, Royal Academy, London). Both are unfinished. Thereafter he eschewed relief-carving altogether, leaving the field to more traditionally minded sculptors, such as Andrea and Jacopo Sansovino. ¶ Other sculptors in the mid-15th century used the relief regularly to depict narratives on tombs, altarpieces or pulpits. With greater or less success they introduced perspective —either linear or aerial into their *mises-en-scène*. Mino da Fiesole, Antonio

Rossellino, Verrocchio and Pollaiolo constructed veritable boxes of fictive space into which to set their figures at various levels as appropriate on a sloping floor. Benedetto da Maiano in a series of scenes depicting the Legend of St. Francis on a pulpit in Santa Croce was bolder yet and canted the architectural scenario at an angle to the front plane, thus introducing an altogether more sophisticated *modus operandi*. He was among the first to use clay models for such scenes, probably in view of their complexity and the need to ensure that the perspectival illusion would look convincing (models: Victoria & Albert Museum, London, three; Staatliche Museen, Berlin, one). The newly confident rendering of space led the way to the High Renaissance treatment of the relief, notably by Andrea Sansovino in his two large panels on the marble cladding of the exterior of the Holy House at Loreto, the *Annunciation* and the *Adoration of the Shepherds*. ¶ Thereafter, around 1540, a reaction set in, led by the Florentine Mannerist sculptor Bandinelli, who was probably influenced by Bronzino, a painter at the court of the Medici. The negation, even contradiction, of fictive space—and thus of realistic appearances—characterizes Bandinelli's reliefs, for example the panel on his monument to Giovanni delle Bande Nere (Piazza San Lorenzo, Florence). His vertical panels of individual *Prophets* that adorn in large numbers the surround of the choir enclosure in Florence Cathedral, though ambitiously and curiously posed (some even nude and seen from behind), are also set against a neutral background, as though to proclaim once more that they are part of an architectural ensemble. This is the opposite of the approach that had held sway for the last 150 years, for the standard Renaissance relief had attempted to approximate a view through a pretended window in the wall. ¶ This tendency is even more pronounced in reliefs by Pierino da Vinci, the sculptor-nephew of Leonardo (but one who was too young ever to have met him) and a great admirer in the middle of the 16th century of the elderly Michelangelo. Pierino's classic panel is supposed to depict the hideous fate of Ugolino della Gherardesca devouring his sons, a scene from Dante's *Inferno* (bronze cast, Chatsworth House, Derbyshire; terracotta and wax casts, Ashmolean Museum, Oxford; others in Florence). Apart from a hag flying in the sky and grimaces on two of the faces of the assortment of languidly posed nude males assembled on a river-bank around a father-figure who resembles Michelangelo's *Moses* in undress, one would be hard put to interpret the actual narrative or horrible context of the historical event. Indeed, Pierino was forced to inscribe the full literary reference on the rocks of the river-bank in front in order to point the spectator in the right direction. The sculptor even dispensed with any visual remnant of a prison interior, such as would have stimulated an earlier sculptor to demonstrate his expertise in rendering linear perspective. To a less marked degree, Cellini also preferred the irreal atmosphere engendered by inconsistent perspective and scale of figures when he came to model his panel of *Perseus rescuing Andromeda* to enhance his monumental group of *Perseus and Medusa* in 1554 (Loggia dei Lanzi, Piazza della Signoria, Florence). Both these reliefs, as well as a number of others by artists such as Tribolo, are so close in feeling to contemporary painting that they may justifiably be labelled as Mannerist, even though there is some doubt as to the applicability of the term to the art of sculpture. ¶ Vincenzo Danti, another sculptor who might be regarded as a Mannerist, took a different approach. In his large bronze relief for an altar frontal in a chapel designed by Bronzino in the Palazzo della Signoria, *Moses and the Brazen Serpent* (c. 1570, Bargello, Florence), he reverts to an approximation of Donatello's late style, evoking a frenzied mêlée of people, deftly modeled in low relief and not 'finished' in the traditional sense, as a foil for the majestic central figure of Moses. The effect of agitated movement suggests the drama of the event, though at the expense of easy legibility. ¶ Legibility was to become an overriding criterion both for sculpture and painting, following the edicts of the Council of Trent, promulgated in 1564, that launched the Catholic Counter-Reformation. A renewed attention to the didactic approach—similar to the mediaeval idea of pictures as the 'Bible of the Poor'—was required and breaches were severely investigated by the Inquisition. Accordingly, when Giambologna (1525–1608), court sculptor to the Medici, was called upon by a Genoese patron to produce a series of panels depicting the Passion of Christ, he took the matter of legibility very seriously. He reverted to an exaggerated rendering of the 15th century idea of creating an illusion of a 'spatial box', using rapidly converging orthogonals in the architectural settings to make a spectator subconsciously feel a close observer of the scene. He carefully took into account the low viewpoint of a spectator standing on the floor of the chapel for which they were intended, employing in his preliminary models (some of which survive in the Victoria & Albert Museum, London) a strip of wood with a wedge-shaped cross-section nailed on to the back-board to provide a firm receding floor surface, just as Ghiberti, Donatello, Verrocchio and Pollaiolo had been used to do. When a grid pattern suggesting recession had been inscribed on its surface (usually rationalised as a layout of rectangular paving stones), the sculptor would people it with figures of diminishing sizes, according to their purported distance from the eye. Also following Alberti, Giambologna adhered to the principle of isocephaly, whereby all the heads—however far away—were contrived to come up to much the same level. Giambologna modelled his figures in compact blocks, divided from each other before open vistas into the depths of the architectural setting or landscape. To right and left of the foreground, the tallest figures modelled almost in fully three dimensions, lean right out into real space, so as to provide satisfactory views from the diagonals, thus catering for, indeed encouraging, the movement of spectators round the walls of the chapel.

Some Florentine Painted Madonna Reliefs

Ulrich Middeldorf

La scultura e la pittura per il vero sono sorelle, nate di un padre, che è il disegno, in un sol parto et ad un tempo, e non precedono l'una all'altra.[1]

The following essay is a small contribution to a vast problem: the relation between painting and sculpture. Artists and writers of the Italian Renaissance discussed it almost *ad nauseam*. It is of interest to us to verify how their theoretical views were translated into practice.[2] ¶ So much of the polychromy of Renaissance sculpture has been lost or spoilt—by time, by neglect, by prejudice—that has become difficult to visualize what the sculptures originally looked like. That they were polychromed far into the sixteenth century must be taken for granted, though a systematic study would be useful .[3] Here the special case of the plastic materials, clay, stucco, and cartapesta[4] will be considered. If even marble, which as a material has its own value and beauty, was thought to need at least partial coloring and gilding,[5] how much more would this be the case with these mean and indifferent materials. Of course, the sculpture came first and then the coloring. We shall see, however, that occasionally the painter completely took over so that reliefs and pictures have become undistinguishable and interchangeable.¶ Terracotta was a material one did not care to show, and we had better realize that all those terracotta sculptures now stripped of their coloring are far from looking like their original selves.[6] Of course, the della Robbias attended to the polychromy of their sculpture with such perfect technique that it still glories in its old coloring.[7] A famous instance of the collaboration of a sculptor and a painter is the lunette with the *Coronation of the Virgin* over the door of Sant'Egidio in Florence, which was modeled by Dello Delli and painted in 1424 by Bicci di Lorenzo.[8] ¶ Not always was the coloring polychrome. There are cases of gilding—for instance, the tomb of the Beato Pacifico in the Frari in Venice[9] or the lavabo in the cloister of the Certosa of Pavia, modeled by Amadeo and gilded in 1466 by his brother Protasio.[10] The two busts by Alessandro Vittoria in the National Gallery in Washington still had traces of gilding,[11] which today have disappeared. Two additional works by Alessandro Vittoria can be mentioned, the terracotta busts in the museum of the *Seminario* in Venice, one painted a dull, darkish green to imitate bronze, and one white to imitate marble. Both mimetic practices must have been quite common and can be documented by other examples.¶ We also have written proof for them. In an inventory of the Medici collection of 1553 ff., we find "una Carità di terra cotta in color di metallo."[12] In 1444 a certain Giovanni da Roma furnished for the façade of the church of Sant'Antonio in Cremona "quasdam figuras terrecoctas ad fornacem et factas ad modum marmoris."[13] Does this mean that they were painted white? This was certainly the case with the figures on the catafalque for the funeral of Michelangelo[14] and with Benedetto da Maiano's *Madonna dell'Ulivo* in the cathedral of Prato, which is described by Vasari as "di terra, lavorata tanto bene, che così fatta senza altro colore è bella quanto se fusse di marmo."[15] Of course, a terracotta left raw would have clashed badly with the marble relief of a *Pietà* which decorated the altar underneath. How bad it would have looked is demonstrated by some tombs in the cloister of the Santo in Padua made in the form of stone tabernacles which house terracotta busts attributed to Fancesco Segala. The busts have lost their coloring, and with it their protection from the weather, and look pretty miserable with their ugly color and corroded surfaces.¶ Stucco required the same treatment as terracotta, and sculptures fashioned in it were invariably colored.[16] Among the many stuccos and terracottas after Madonna reliefs by Donatello and his followers, there are a few with well-preserved polychromy; as examples may serve a small tabernacle in the Victoria and Albert Museum possibly painted by Paolo Schiavo[17] and one in the art market in Florence. In the lunette of the latter the *Man of Sorrows* is painted. Often the Dove of the Holy Ghost is found in this place. The composition of this piece is known in a number of terracottas and stuccos, the best one in the Victoria and Albert Museum.[18] The example there has unfortunately lost its polychromy, while ours is carefully painted and gilt, with the gold heavily tooled. The slightly pedantic richness of its ornamental decoration denotes a special taste which is also found in stuccos and terracottas after other masters. One might call them the "overdecorated" variety and ask to what whims or to what commercial speculation they owe their existence. They even have plastic decorations added[19] and often come in highly elaborate frames.[20] ❡ A phenomenon that should interest the economic historian is the prodigious production of polychromed Madonna reliefs of a handy size during the fifteenth century in Florence. The appearance of these reliefs is virtually limited to Florence; in Siena there were some; elsewhere none except occasional pieces. The Florentine products must also have been very saleable abroad; they are to be found nearly everywhere in Italy. One might suspect special workshops, perhaps those of some potters, to have turned them out, but there does not seem to be any specific evidence for this. Probably these pieces were the well-paying by-products of the workshops of the great masters, whose terracottas and marbles were used as patterns. At first this production clustered around Ghiberti, though we do not know of a single piece which, with assurance, could be ascribed to him. Then follow the replicas of the Madonnas of Donatello and his school. ❡ The most flourishing phase of the production, however, centered around Desiderio da Settignano, Antonio Rossellino, Domenico Rosselli, Francesco di Simone Ferrucci, the Master of the Marble Madonnas, Benedetto da Maiano, and to a minor extent Verrocchio. Of course, the della Robbias were great contributors, both with their own compositions and those of others which they glazed. What is so puzzling is the sudden outbreak of this fashion, its almost total disappearance after the lapse of a few generations, and its local circumscription. It was followed, lasting into the sixteenth century, by the equally surprising fad of small terracottas in the round by artists like the Master of the Statuettes of Saint John[21] and the slightly later Master of the Unruly Children.[22] We also find the della Robbias in alliance with them. ❡ Neri di Bicci's *ricordanze*[23] give us a lively insight into the activities of a renowned and busy painter of his time, who collaborated with cabinetmakers like Giuliano da Maiano and with woodcarvers like Don Romualdo, abbot of Candeli.[24] Of Neri we learn that:

In 1454 he colors with the blue and gold "una Nostra Donna da chamera di terra cotta."
In 1454 he describes in detail how he painted "una Nostra Donna di gesso" (stucco).
In 1456 he describes in detail how he painted "una Vergine Maria di rilievo grande di gesso" and its tabernacle.
In 1456 he mentions his connection with Desiderio.
In 1461 he paints and gilds a tabernacle for a Madonna in marble by Desiderio.
In 1464 he makes a large tabernacle for a Madonna in stucco by Desiderio.[25]

It is interesting to know that in almost all cases he also had to take care of the gilding and retouching of the frames. These tabernacle frames actually were an integral part of their polychrome reliefs, which—alas—have often been lost or hopelessly spoiled. They deserve a special study, particularly as famous artists like Giuliano da Maiano are involved. ❡ To illustrate the above, two almost identical, well-preserved Madonna reliefs may serve: one formerly in a private collection in Germany without a frame; the other, formerly in the collection of E. Volpi,[26] still with its original tabernacle frame. They reproduce a composition by Desiderio[27] and certainly have been colored by Neri di Bicci. The reduction of Desiderio's lively face and hands to slightly simpleminded schemes betrays Neri's hand and mind. If more proof were needed, there is a picture by him[28] which repeats the composition with some minor variations, and which breathes the same spirit. ❡ A stucco after another composition by Desiderio, which is best known through a marble in Turin,[29] is a particularly attractive example.[30] It is reasonably well preserved in its original tabernacle. The polychromy follows the usual scheme: the garment of the Virgin is red, her cloak dark blue. On both sides of the Madonna two full-length adoring angels are painted with complete disregard for scale. The frame has elegant proportions almost worthy of Giuliano da Maiano. Its frieze is decorated with garlands and heads of cherubim; the gable shows the half-figure of the blessing God the Father. A half-effaced inscription in excellent lettering, AVE MARIA GRATIA PLENA, completes the picture. Such were Neri di Bicci's finest productions. ❡ As a rule, the painters who colored such reliefs cannot be identified. There is, however, another exception. A painter known as the Pseudo Pier Francesco Fiorentino,[31] though slightly younger, has many similarities to Neri di Bicci. His output was large and repetitive; his works are schematic and artisanlike. He often depended on the ideas of others, such as Filippo Lippi and Pesellino. For the coloring of Madonna reliefs, he qualified through his meticulous technique and the skill with which he handled decorative details – above all flowers. A stucco in the Currier Gallery of Art in Manchester, New Hampshire,[32] which repeats perhaps the most popular Madonna of the century by the young Antonio Rossellino,[33] is certainly colored by him, as comparison with one of his pictures shows.[34] That all this was serial production is proved by the fact that there also exists an almost identical piece, in the Musée Jacquemart-André in Paris.[35]¶ This story comes full circle—with a curious twist, however. Another extremely well-known composition by Antonio Rossellino[36] was copied in a picture, if Berenson was right, by the *real* Pierfrancesco Fiorentino.[37] This fact might have induced Berenson to reconsider his distinction between the real and "pseudo," at least for this picture. Two technical details may illustrate how closely the arts of painting and sculpture are interwoven in these works. The gilding of the haloes and of decorative details like borders is often tooled as in pictures. And often the colors of the garments are not applied evenly, but are graded from deeper tones in the depths of the folds to lighter ones on the ridges, which enhances the modeling. In a photograph this trick cannot be seen; but its effect does show. Which brings us back to the quotation from Vasari that introduced this essay.

NOTES

1. Giorgio Vasari, *Le vite de' più eccellenti pittori, scultori ed architettori*, ed. Gaetano Milanesi (Firenze 1906), 1, p. 103 (hereafter cited as Vasari-Milanesi); idem, *Le vite de' più eccellenti pittori, scultori ed architettori, nelle redazioni del 1550 e 1568*, ed. Rosanna Bettarini and Paola Barocchi (Firenze 1966–71), 1, p.26.

2. The latest contribution to the subject, which discusses its main aspects, is by John Pope-Hennessy, "The interaction of painting and sculpture in Florence in the fifteenth century." *The Journal of the Royal Society of Arts*, 117, 1969, pp. 406–24.

3. I have the suspicion that the statues and reliefs of the campanile of Santa Maria del Fiore originally were painted a bright yellow ochre so as to appear gilded, as are the statues in the background of Botticelli's *Calumny of Apelles*. They are entirely covered by a thin layer of some earth, except for patches where it has flaked off. This could easily be a faded yellow earth. For yellow and gold to be indistinguishable at some distance is a common experience. The problem would be worth a chemical analysis.

4. In these pages stucco and terracotta will not be treated as distinct from each other. Sometimes it is quite difficult to obtain information as to which of the two materials forms the medium of a given piece. The two materials did not differ in the process of production. A squeeze from a mold is taken as easily in one as in the other. Both can be, and were, retouched afterwards. The quality of stucco varies greatly from a soft, crumbly substance to a hard, marblelike one. There are also squeezes in cartapesta and in leather. The latter are quite rare, and the surfaces of those I have seen do not allow any conclusions concerning original coloring.

5. The polychromy of bronzes since antiquity is a special case. Of some interest is the information on the silvering of the faces and hands of Donatello's bronzes in Padua quoted by James H. Beck, *Mitteilungen des Kunsthistorischen Instituts in Florenz*, 14, 1969–70, p. 459, n. 8. Sculpture composed of various materials, e.g. Verrocchio's Medici tomb, is again another matter.

6. Jacob Burckhardt, "Skuptur der Renaissance," *Gesamtausgabe*, 1934, 13, p. 197, states that certain terracottas were left unpainted, without giving reasons. His piece is perhaps the best ever written on Renaissance sculpture, and his views otherwise deserve the closest attention.

7. As another aside it might be added that some later della Robbia products, which try to imitate the variety of color of painting, have faces and hands as well as other areas unglazed. The reason for this was, of course, that these parts were intended to be naturalistically painted. Time and lack of understanding have frequently removed this paint, giving the figures unusually dark complexions.

8. For the literature, see Walter and Elisabeth Paatz, *Die Kirchen von Florenz*, (Frankfurt-am-Main 1940-54), 4, pp. 13, 41; Ulrich Middeldorf, "Dello Delli and The Man of Sorrows in the Victoria and Albert Museum," *The Burlington Magazine*, 78 1941, pp. 71–78; and more recently, although not convincing, James H. Beck, "Masaccio's Early Career as a Sculptor," *The Art Bulletin*, 53, 1971, pp. 177–95.

9. Pietro Paoletti, *L'architettura e la scultura del rinascimento a Venezia*, (Venezia 1893), 1, p. 185 n., quotes Marino Sanuto.

10. Carlo Magenta, *La Certosa di Pavia*, (Milano 1897), p. 454.

11. Theodor von Frimmel, "Terracottabüsten des Alessandro Vittoria im K.K. Oesterr. Museum f. Kunst u. Industrie," *Mitteilungen des K.K. Oesterreichischen Museums für Kunst und Industrie*, 11, no. 129, (Wien 1896), p. 188; National Gallery of Art, *Summary Catalogue of European Paintings and Sculpture*, Washington, D.C., pp. 173–174, nos. A 1666 and A 1667; illustrated National Gallery of Art, *European Paintings and Sculpture*, (Washington, D.C., 1968), p. 153.

12. Eugène Muentz, *Les collections d'antiques formées par les Médicis au XVIe siècle, Mémoires de l'Académie des Inscriptions et Belles-lettres*, (Paris 1895), p. 59.

13. Alfredo Puerari, *Le tarsie del Platina*, (Milano 1967), pp. 13, 131.

14. Allan Marquand, *Benedetto and Santi Buglioni*, (Princeton 1921), p. 215; Vasari-Milanesi, 7, pp. 298, 303.

15. Vasari-Milanesi, 3, p. 344.

16. There is, however, a type of stucco which is evenly covered by a thin brown stain. This type mostly reproduces more ambitious reliefs, e.g. parts of the Doors of Paradise or marbles by Benedetto da Maiano. Occasionally they are claimed to be models. They must, however, be later casts, since I have seen some after Giovanni Bologna's Passion reliefs. They are usually very well molded and close to the originals.

17. Philip Pouncey, "A Painted Frame by Paolo Schiavo," *The Burlington Magazine*, 88, 1946, p. 228; John Pope-Hennessy, *Catalogue of Italian Sculpture in the Victoria and Albert Museum*, (London 1964), 1, p. 83, n. 68.

18. Pope-Hennessy, *Catalogue of Italian Sculpture*, I, p. 77, no. 64.

19. They are frequent but are rarely found reproduced. For example, see Allan Marquand, "Antonio Rossellino's Madonna of the Candelabra," *Art in America*, 7, 1919, pp. 198-206.

20. For an example (after Rossellino) in the Victoria and Albert Museum, see Pope-Hennessy, 1, pp. 133–34, no. III.

21. Ibid., pp. 191-96.

22. Frida Schottmüller, *Die Bildwerke in Stein, Holz, Ton und Wachs (Bildwerke des Kaiser Friedrich-Museums: Die italienischen und spanischen Bildwerke der Renaissance und des Barock*, I, (Berlin and Leipzig 1933), pp. 157-59.

23. These *ricordanze* were unfortunately never completely published; but see Filippo Baldinucci, *Notizie dei professori del disegno...* (per cura di F. Ranalli), (Firenze 1845–47); reprint, 1975; Vasari-Milanesi, 2, pp. 69–90; Giovanni Poggi, "Le Ricordanze di Neri di Bicci (1453–1475)," *Il Vasari*, 1, 1927/1928, pp. 317–38, 3, 1930, pp. 133–53, 222–234, 4, 1931, pp. 181–202. Since these pages were written, the complete text of the *ricordanze* has been published. See Neri Di Bicci, *Le Ricordanze (10 marzo 1453–24 aprile 1475)*, (Bruno Santi, Pisa, Edizioni Marlin, 1976).

24. Poggi, "Le Ricordanze di Neri di Bicci (1453–1475)," *Il Vasari*, 3 pp. 227, 231, 4, p. 189; Vasari-Milanesi, 2, p. 86, n. 7. He is mentioned in 1456 and 1469. This prolific carver of crucifixes probably is responsible for some of those published by Margrit Lisner, *Holzkruzifixe in Florenz und in der Toskana von der Zeit um 1300 bis zum frühen Cinquecento*, (München 1970).

25. Poggi, "Le Ricordanze di Neri di Bicci (1453–1475)," *Il Vasari*, 1, pp. 329, 332–33; 3, pp. 233–34; 4, p. 194; Clarence Kennedy, "Documenti inediti su Desiderio da Settignano e la sua famiglia," *Rivista d'Arte*, 12, 1930, pp. 274, 276.

26. New York, *American Art Galleries*, Nov. 21, 1916, n. 710.

27. See Pope-Hennessy, 1, pp. 142–46, no. 117, who discusses the various replicas also in pictures.

28. In the museum of Dijon.

29. Noemi Gabrielli, *Galleria Sabauda. Maestri italiani*, (Torino 1971), p. 261. I do not believe it to be a forgery. This is not the place to enter into a discussion, which would have to concern itself with fundamentals of the production of marbles in the Quattrocento. See also Ida Cardellini, *Desiderio da Settignano*, (Milano 1962), pp. 286 ff., where other polychromed specimens are reproduced.

30. I have seen the piece in the art market in Florence.

31. Ulrich Thieme and Felix Becker, *Allgemeines Lexikon der Bildenden Künstler von der Antike bis zur Gegenwart*, (Leipzig 1907-50), 37, 1950, p. 281.

32. Formerly in the Acquavella Galleries in New York. See W.R. Valentiner, *Catalogue of an Exhibition of Italian Gothic and early Renaissance Sculptures*, (Detroit, The Detroit Institute of Arts, 1938), no. 4; Valentiner has identified the Pseudo Pierfrancesco Fiorentino as the author of the coloring of both pieces. I am grateful to David S. Brooke for the photograph.

33. See Pope-Hennessy, 1, p. 133, no. III.

34. The picture is in a private collection; the author thanks the owner for permission to publish the photograph.

35. Georges E. Lafenestre, at al., *Le Musée Jacquemart-André*, (Paris 1914), pp. 89–90 and illustration.

36. See Pope-Hennessy, 1, pp. 132–133, no. 110.

37. Bernard Berenson, *Homeless Paintings of the Renaissance*, (London 1969), pp. 177, 318.

Catalogue

DONATELLO
Florentine, 1386-1464

1. *Virgin and Child with Four Angels*

Polychromed stucco in original gessoed, painted and gilded frame, 38.5 cm. (15⅛ inches) in height, c. 1420-25

BIBLIOGRAHY: A. M. Migliarini, *Museo di sculture del Risorgimento raccolto e posseduto da Ottavio Gigli*, Florence, 1858, pl. xxxvii.; W. Bode, *Denkmäler der Renaissance-Sculptor Toscanas*, Munich, 1892–1905, p. 21; W. Bode, *Florentiner Bildhauer der Renaissance*, Berlin, 1902, pp. 19, 101–102.; Lord Balcarres, *Donatello*, London, 1903, p. 184; A. Meyer, *Donatello*, Bielefeld and Leipzig, 1903, p. 60; F. Schottmüller, *Donatello*, Munich, 1904, p. 20; P. Schubring, *Donatello*, Stuttgart and Berlin, 1907, pp. xxviii, 82, and 198; W. Bode, *Florentine Sculptors of the Renaissance*, London, 1908, pp. 59–60: M. Cruttwell, *Donatello*, London, 1911, p. 135; A. Colasanti, *Donatello*, Milan, 1931, p. 86; H. Kauffman, *Donatello*, Berlin, 1935, p. 218, n. 210; L. Goldscheider, *Donatello*, London, 1941, p. 44.; W. Hildburgh, "A Marble Relief Attributable to Donatello, and Some Associated Stuccos," *Art Bulletin* 30, 1946, pp. 11-19; H. W. Janson, "The Hildburgh Relief: Original or Copy?" *Art Bulletin* 30, 1946, pp. 143–145; W. Hildburgh, Letter to the Editor, *Art Bulletin* 30, 1946, pp. 244-246; H. W. Janson, *Donatello*, Princeton, 1957, p. 242; J. Pope-Hennessy and R. Lightbown, *Catalogue of the Italian Sculpture in the Victoria and Albert Museum*, London, 1964, pp. 91–95; C. Avery, "Donatello's Madonnas Reconsidered," *Apollo*, 1986, pp. 174–182; C. Avery, *Donatello*, Florence, 1991, p. 54; A. Rosenauer, *Donatello*, Milan, 1993, p. 314.

EXHIBITED: The Robert Lehman Collection, The Metropolitan Museum of Art, New York, 1997–1999.

This extremely famous composition is known in three variants: 1) the present work; 2) a closely associated marble relief (Victoria and Albert Museum, London; A.98-1956); and 3) another pigmented stucco version in which the standing figures are saints rather than angels (Victoria and Albert Museum, London; 93-1882). Until the discovery and publication of the marble version in 1946, the composition was universally regarded as a major early work by Donatello. Among the scholars supporting this view were Bode, Schottmüller, Cruttwell, Goldscheider, and Kauffmann. Bode was especially lavish in his praise, writing: "This rich composition of six full-length figures is so admirably grouped and so wonderfully effective in its setting in the noble vaulted architecture, that the small relief must undoubtedly be ranked as one of the finest among the master's early works" (1908, pp. 59–60). According to Bode, it was "unquestionably the work of Donatello's own hand." (*ibid.*, p. 13) ¶ All scholars agreed that the relief was made in the mid or late 1420s. In support of this view, they pointed to the many similarities of the composition with contemporary pieces by Donatello, especially the *Feast of Herod* (Baptistery, Siena), and the relief of the *Assuntà* for the Brancacci Monument (S. Angelo a Nilo, Naples). Indeed, as many have observed, the logical organization of the space, achieved in large part by the clear recession of the planes of the architecture, resembles the space of the *Feast of Herod*. Two other notable points of comparison with that work are 1) the viol-playing angel in the foreground, who strongly resembles the musician in the middle distance of the *Feast*, and 2) the gesture of the standing angel on the right, which is like that of the figure immediately to Herod's right in the Siena relief. Furthermore, as has been widely remarked, the profiles of the angels in the present work are comparable to the profiles of the figures both in the *Assuntà* and in the *Tabernacle of the Sacrament* (Basilica of St. Peter's, Rome). As evidence of the present work's early date, scholars have also cited the similarity of the composition with that of the central panel of Masaccio's *Pisa Altarpiece* (National Gallery, London), and have compared the architecture in the relief with that of Masaccio's *Trinity Altarpiece* (S. Maria Novella, Florence). ¶ In 1946 Hildburgh published a marble variant which was then in his collection and later donated to the Victoria and Albert Museum. Both Janson and Pope-Hennessy rejected the marble as an autograph work by Donatello, arguing that it was instead a derivative work from the mid-fifteenth century. Assuming that the marble must have served as the model for the other versions, they likewise dismissed the stucco versions of the relief. For Pope-Hennessy and Janson, the composition and all three of its variants were part of a relatively large group of works made in the style of Donatello by a variety of anonymous artists in the middle of the fif-

teenth century. ❡ However, there are two strong counter arguments in support of its attribution to Donatello. First, the Hall version was not cast from the marble, as Janson and Pope-Hennessy believed. There are subtle but important differences between the marble and the Hall version. For instance, in the upper part of the Hall version, the details of the architecture on the left side are in very low relief, and yet the corresponding details on the right side are not in relief, but are painted instead. This is not the case in the marble version, where the details on both the left and the right are in low relief. This difference alone indicates that the stucco cannot have been cast from the marble. Moreover, the Hall version throughout is the finer of the two in its detail and interpretative character. Second, there is compelling evidence that the composition certainly existed by the early 1430s at the latest. As Rosenauer has observed, the relief seems to have influenced Filippo Lippi's *Cini Madonna* (Fondazione Cini, Venice), a work from the beginning of his career. Moreover, Kanter has attributed the angels in the spandrels of the frame of the Hall version to the Pseudo-Ambrogio di Baldese, a minor master active in Florence in the early quattrocento.[1] The present stucco thus seems to have been made in Florence sometime before Donatello's departure for Padua in 1443. In these circumstances, given the strong Donatellesque character of the composition, it is difficult to believe that the stucco records a composition by any artist other than the master himself. The Hall version is thus the earliest of the three variants; and it is likely to have been made in Donatello's workshop as a direct cast from a relief by the artist. Bode and others believed that the Hall stucco was cast from a bronze rather than a marble relief and they suggested that this relief might possibly have served as a tabernacle door, even, conceivably, that of the *Tabernacle of the Sacrament* in St. Peter's. Both hypotheses deserve careful reconsideration. ❡ The provenance of the Hall version is noteworthy. The piece is documented in the collection of Ottavio Gigli, Florence , in the middle of the nineteenth century. (This collection was a source for many of the Italian sculptures in the Victoria and Albert Museum.) The relief later passed to the legendary dealer, Stefano Bardini, from whom it was purchased by Prof. Werner Weisbach, Berlin. Subsequently, the sculpture belonged to Dr. F.F. Nord at Fordham University, New York.

1 I am grateful to Dr. Laurence Kanter for discussing this attribution with me. On the Pseudo-Ambrogio di Baldese, see L. Kanter et al., *Painting and Illumination in Early Renaissance Florence 1300-1500*, exh. cat., The Metropolitan Museum of Art, New York, 1994, pp. 318ff., with additional bibliography.

LUCA DELLA ROBBIA
(Florence 1399–1482 Florence)

2. *Madonna and Child*

Polychromed and gilded stucco and wood, 37 cm. (14½ inches) in diameter, circa 1440

BIBLIOGRAPHY: M. Reymond, "La Madone Corsini de Luca della Robbia," *Rivista d'arte* II, 1904, pp. 93–100; P. Schubring, *Luca della Robbia und seine Familie*, Bielefeld, 1921, p. 81; A. Marquand, *Luca della Robbia*, Princeton, 1914, nos. 85–93; J. Pope-Hennessy, *Luca della Robbia*, Oxford, 1980, pp. 62, 25; R. Kecks, *Madonna und Kind*, Berlin, 1988, p. 90; G. Gentilini, *I della Robbia*, Milan, 1992, pp. 48, 98–99.

Universally dated around 1440, this composition was among the very first images of the Madonna and Child that Luca della Robbia created. While no autograph example in marble or glazed terracotta survives, the composition is recorded in a series of stucco reliefs, nearly all of which are circular and which vary between 28 and 37 cm. The largest and finest of these seem to have been produced in Luca's shop, working from his molds. It was an unusually popular image, and versions were made as late as the sixteenth century. Sir John Pope-Hennessy has written about the work: "In close proximity to the *Friedrichstein Madonna*, Luca seems to have evolved a second composition, known, from a later version in enameled terracotta, as the *Corsini Madonna*. From the examples that survive—mainly in painted stucco, though a small version in stone was inserted over the lintel of a pietra serena doorway in Santa Maria Nuova—we must suppose that it was very popular. It shows the Virgin and Child in a circular concave field, and at the time it was produced, about 1440, it represented a strikingly progressive solution of the geometry of the tondo form" (*op.cit.*, p. 62). ¶ Other examples of the work survive in the Musée Jacquemart-André, Paris; the Museo Bardini, Florence; Santa Maria in Castello, Genoa, and elsewhere.

LUCA DELLA ROBBIA
(Florence 1399–1482 Florence)

3. *Madonna and Child*

Cartapesta, 50.8 x 34.9 cm. (20 x 13¾ inches), c. 1460

BIBLIOGRAPHY: M. Crutwell, *Luca della Robbia*, London, 1902, pp 111–113; P. Schubring, *Die Italienische Plastik des Quattrocento*, Munich, 1919, pp. 82–85; A. Marquand, *Luca della Robbia*, Princeton, 1914, nos. 92, 93, pp. 141-145; 236–240; J. Pope-Hennessy, *Luca della Robbia*, Oxford, 1980, pp. 66, 245–46; G. Gentilini, *I della Robbia*, Milan, 1992, pp. 104, 118–19, 132.

The most sacred image in Renaissance Florence was a painting of the Madonna and Child that was housed at the church of Santa Maria in Impruneta, a small village a few kilometers from the city. Known as the Madonna di Impruneta, the image was believed to have the power to control weather. At times of drought or flood, as well as during other emergencies, the painting was brought to Florence in a sacred procession and placed in the Duomo, where the Virgin was propitiated in a special mass and ceremony. ¶ In 1439 Antonio degli Agli was appointed *piovano* of Santa Maria di Impruneta, and under his leadership, the church was substantially rebuilt over the course of the next three decades. To execute the program of modernization, degli Agli hired a team of artists, most notably Michelozzo and Luca della Robbia. In the 1450s they erected a pair of aedicula chapels flanking the high altar; one chapel housed the miraculous image of the Madonna, and the other, a relic of the true cross. The Chapel of the Madonna is decorated on two sides with a frieze of grape vine, depicted in enamelled terracotta; at the center of each frieze is an identical low relief of the Madonna and Child. The present sculpture is derived directly from those reliefs. ¶ In the relief, the Madonna cradles the Child in her arms, her head bowed to touch His head with her cheek, while the Child leans forward with His arms raised and rests His head on the Madonna's upper chest. The perfect contentment of the Child is evident, as is the shadow of anxiety on the Madonna's face, troubled by her foreknowledge of His sacrifice and death. ¶ The present work is in painted cartapesta, a form of papier mâché. This was the humblest material for sculpture, and like stucco and terracotta was frequently used for the replication of popular religious images. ¶ Sir John Pope-Hennessy has written: "In the history of Quattrocento sculpture Luca della Robbia's *Madonnas* occupy a place like that of the *Madonnas* of Giovanni Bellini in the history of painting, in that they enable us to follow the response of one artist to the formal and emotional challenge of a single theme. Conceived on a level of unwavering seriousness, they partake of the mimetic nature of the Cantoria carvings, and their inventiveness is the by-product of an art that was rooted in real life. The angels who diffidently bow their heads, like servers at the Mass, before the Oxford *Madonna of the Humility*; the Child in the *Corsini Madonna* pulling at the Virgin's veil with a possessive arm; the Virgin in the *Friedrichstein Madonna* gazing at the Child with half-closed eyes; the Virgin of the two *Madonnas* at Impruneta clutching the Child against her breast as though protecting Him from harm; the Virgin of the *Altman Madonna* looking on in reluctant acquiescence as the Child's mission is affirmed; the majestic *Madonna* in the Innocenti pointing to the inscription that asserts her own humility; the nervous, playful Child of the *Madonna of the Apple* in Berlin—all these proceed from observation, but observation raised to a new power" (*op.cit.*, p. 66).

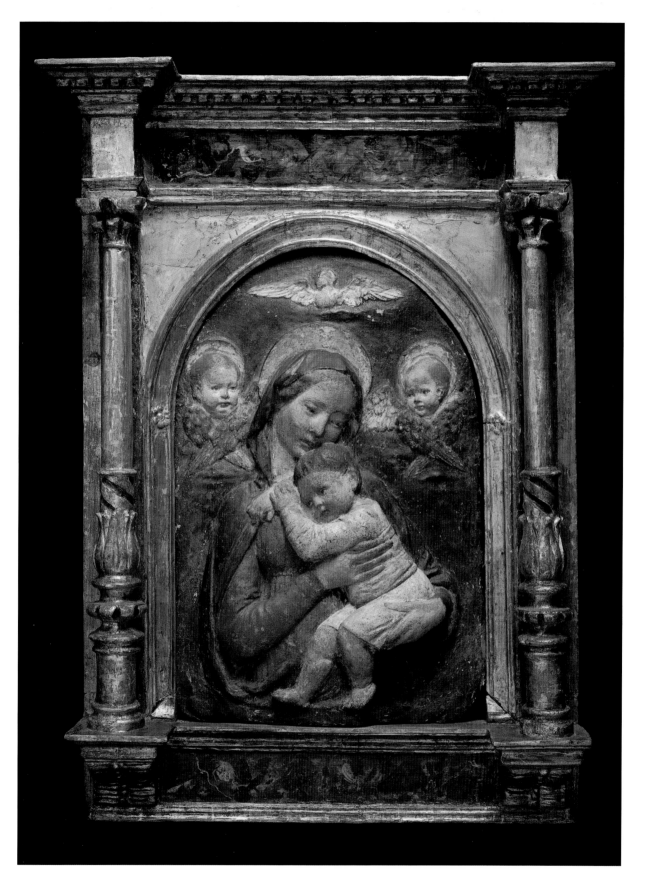

ANTONIO ROSSELLINO
(Florence 1427–1479 Florence)

4. *Madonna of the Candelabra*

Polychromed stucco, 81 x 55.5 cm. (32 x 22 inches),
c. 1457-1461

BIBLIOGRAPHY: A. Marquand, "Antonio Rossellino's Madonna of the Candelabra," *Art in America* VII, 1918-1919, pp. 198-206; H. Gottschalk, *Antonio Rossellino*, Liegnitz, 1930, p. 94; J. Pope-Hennessy and R. Lightbown, *Catalogue of Italian Sculpture in the Victoria and Albert Museum*, London, 1964, I, no. 110, pp. 132-33; D. Kaezmarzyk, "La *Madonna dei Candelabri* d'Antonio Rossellino," *Bulletin du Musée national du Varsovie* XII, 1971, pp. 55-58; J. Pope-Hennessy, "The Altman Madonna," in *The Study and Criticism of Italian Sculpture*, New York, 1980, pp. 146-47; R. Kecks, *Madonna und Kind*, Berlin 1988, p. 102; J. Pope-Hennessy, *Italian Renaissance Sculpture*, 4th ed., London, 1996, p. 374.

The relief depicts the Madonna and Child seated in an elaborate gilded throne. The finials of the throne terminate in flaming candelabra, and draped from these are a swag of flowers and two strings of coral beads. The Madonna, turned slightly to the right, holds the Child atop a golden pillow on her lap. With her right hand she supports His feet, and with her left she pulls her mantel up around His back and shoulders. The Child innocently clutches a swallow in his hands. ¶ No marble original of the relief survives; but there are numerous versions in a variety of media, including stucco, terracotta, cartapesta and Istrian stone. As Pope-Hennessy has noted, "the composition seems to have enjoyed unusual popularity in the fifteenth-century." ¶ It is easy to see why. The acutely observed and deeply affecting language of gestures, the beautifully rendered contrast of expressions, and the extraordinary spatial realism are all of the greatest sophistication. ¶ Antonio Rossellino was the author of the relief, as Marquand, Gottschalk, Pope-Hennessy and others have noted. One need only compare it with the *Altman Madonna* and the *Morgan Madonna* to see the indubitable certainty of the attribution. The pose of the Madonna is a near-mirror image of these other Madonnas, and the head of the baby is extremely close in form to the infant's in the Altman relief. The treatment of costume, gesture and space is also highly alike. Both the *Altman Madonna* and the *Morgan Madonna* are believed to have been made circa 1457–1461. It is likely the *Madonna of the Candelabra* dates from the same period. ¶ The present stucco is among the largest and finest versions of the relief in the world. Its size and quality distinguish it from the copies and aftercasts of the composition. As such, the stucco is surely by Antonio Rossellino, not a follower. ¶ The polychromy can also be securely attributed. The palette exactly matches that of Neri di Bicci, the Florentine painter (1418–1492). One need only compare the present work with Neri's *Assumption of the Virgin* (1458; Toronto, National Gallery of Canada) and his *Coronation of the Virgin* (1459; Florence, Academia). For example, the intense yellow of the infant's hair is identical with that of the hair of St. Michael in the *Coronation*. ¶ As is well-known, Neri di Bicci's account book, the *Ricordanze*, survives and shows that he painted stucco reliefs of the Madonna and Child on a frequent basis. A typical entry for one of these reads:

> Martedì a dì 13 di febraio 1458 [1459 modern style] Richordo ch`el sopradetto dì vendei a Bendetto d'Andrea di Bosi tintore uno cholmo da camera fatto al'anticha chon una Vergine Maria di gesso di pocho rilievo cholorita; el tabernacholo messo d'oro fine dinanzi e da llato d'oro di metà e d'azuro di Magnia; ornato e fatto a ogni mia ispcsa di c[i]ò bisognia a detto cholmo e per llo legniame: in tuto me ne debe dare d'achordo l. trenta, fatto el sopradetto dì. Posto che de' dare a libro D ac. 53.

As Neri's entries indicate, such reliefs were typically placed in gilded wood classicizing tabernacles and were intended to be located in domestic interiors, especially the bedroom.

DESIDERIO DA SETTIGNANO
(Settignano c. 1430–Florence 1464)

5. *Madonna and Child*

Polychromed stucco, 70.5 x 46.5 cm. (27¾ x 18¼ inches), c. 1455–1460

BIBLIOGRAPHY: W. Bode, *Italienische Bildhauer der Renaissance*, Berlin, 1887, p. 55; W. Bode, *Denkmäler der Renaissance-Sculptor Toscanas*, Munich, 1892–1905, pp. 93–94; L. Planiscig, *Desiderio da Settignano*, Vienna, 1942, pp. 13, 41; I. Cardellini, *Desiderio da Settignano*, Milan, 1962, p. 144; C. Avery, *Florentine Renaissance Sculpture*, London, 1970, p. 109; N. Gabrielli, *Galleria Sabauda; maestri italiani*, Turin, 1971, p. 261; Neri di Bicci, *Le Ricordanze*, ed. B. Santi, Pisa, 1976, p. 239; A. M. Schulz, "Desiderio da Settignano," *Dizionario biografico italiano*, vol. 39, Rome, 1991, pp. 385–390; A. M. Schulz, "Glosses on the Career of Desiderio da Settignano," in S. Bule et al., *Verrocchio and Late Quattrocento Italian Sculpture*, Florence, 1992, p. 186; J. Pope-Hennessy, *Italian Renaissance Sculpture*, London, 1996, p. 375.

The present work is related to the so-called *Turin Madonna* in the Galleria Sabauda: the pose of the Madonna and Child is identical and the measurements correspond. The *Turin Madonna* was first attributed to Desiderio by Bode, whose attribution has been endorsed by Planiscig, Cardellini, Avery, Pope-Hennessy and others. However, Gabrielli and Schulz believe that the Turin marble is a nineteenth-century fake based on a stucco version; yet they too agree that the stuccos originally stem from Desiderio. ¶ Evidently, it was an extraordinarily popular image. Painted stucco versions are extant in several public collections, including the Ashmolean Museum, the Victoria and Albert Museum, the Fogg Art Museum, the Staatliche Museum in Berlin, and the Musée de Lyon. The polychromy of these versions differs significantly. The versions in the Ashmolean and the Victoria and Albert, like the marble in Turin, show the Madonna and Child against a simple background that is adorned solely with a floral swag above. The version in the Fogg Art Museum shows the Madonna and Child in a painted niche. The present version shows them against a starry sky and flanked by angels with the Holy Spirit above. The painting of the Madonna's costume also differs in the various versions. ¶ The present work was pigmented by Neri di Bicci. As in Antonio Rossellino's *Madonna of the Candelabra* (cat. no. 4), the palette exactly corresponds with that of Neri's panel pictures. Moreover, in his *Ricordanze* Neri mentions a stucco version of this composition. The main text of the entry reads as follows:

> Martedì a dì 19 di febraio 1464 [modern style 1465] Richordo ch'el sopradetto dì rendei finito di tutto a Ronbolo d' Andrea di Nofri fa batere l'oro da filare, uno cholmo da chamera grande, drentovi una Nostra Donna di gesso di mano di Disiderio cho Nostro Signiore in chollo ch'è mezo fasciato, el quale tabernacholo e Nostra Donna fu già altra volta dipinto e messo parte d'oro e parte biancho e d'altri cholori e nuovo lo rasi e missi el tabernacholo d'oro fine. (Neri di Bicci, 1976).

Schulz (1992) has observed that this entry postdates Desiderio's death, and she has argued that this proves Desiderio's shop continued to produce stucco versions of his works, even after his death. But this hypothesis is not compelling. What the entry actually records is Neri's complete repainting of the wooden tabernacle that housed the relief. The entry therefore has no bearing on either the date of the stucco version or even the date of Neri's painting of the relief. The *Turin Madonna* is often said to come from the early part of Desiderio's career. But his career was short—little more than a decade—and its chronology is not clear. The relief, therefore, cannot be more precisely dated than c. 1455–1460.

Benedetto da Maiano
(Maiano 1442–1497 Florence)

6A. *God the Father and Two Angels*

Polychromed terracotta, 36.2 cm. (14¼ inches) in height, c. 1489

6B. *Angel of the Annunciation* (overleaf)

Polychromed terracotta, 81.3 cm. (32 inches) in height, c. 1489

BIBLIOGRAPHY: L. Dussler, "A Clay Model by Benedetto da Majano for the Altar in Monte Oliveto Naples," *Burlington Magazine* XLV, July 1924, pp. 21–22; L. Dussler, *Benedetto da Maiano*, Munich, 1924, pp. 21–23, 39–42, 83; R. Pane, *Il Rinascimento nell'Italia meriodinale*, Milan, 1975, vol. I, pp. 235–237; G. Radke, "Benedetto da Maiano and the Use of Full Scale Preparatory Models in the Quattrocento," in S. Bule et al., *Andrea del Verrocchio and Late Quattrocento Italian Sculpture*, Florence, 1992, pp. 217–224; A. Radcliffe, *The Thyssen-Bornemisza Collection. Renaissance and Later Sculpture*, London, 1992, cat. no. 4, pp. 62–67; J. Pope-Hennessy, *Italian Renaissance Sculpture,* 4th ed., London, 1996, pp. 114, 382.

At an undetermined date sometime in the 1480s, Benedetto da Maiano was commissioned to make a large marble altarpiece for the Altar of the Annunciation in the Terranova (later Mastrogiudice) chapel in the church of Monte Oliveto (S. Anna dei Lombardi), Naples (fig. 1). One wall of this chapel was already decorated with a large marble altarpiece carved by Antonio Rossellino around 1470–75. Benedetto's sculpture was intended for the wall facing Rossellino's and was made in direct competition with the earlier altarpiece. Benedetto carved the sculptures of his altarpiece in Florence, finishing the work by September 1489, when the marbles are recorded as ready for shipping. ¶ The two altarpieces represent a highpoint in pictorial sculpture in Quattrocento Florence. Pope-Hennessy has commented: "In two altarpieces carved for Naples it [the barrier between painting and sculpture] is eliminated. The first of these was executed by Antonio Rossellino . . . No previous Renaissance sculptor had faced the problem of constructing a monumental pictorial relief, and had the scene no other merits, its spatial content . . . would entitle Antonio to a place among the most resourceful sculptors of his time. A corresponding altarpiece with the Annunciation was completed fifteen years later by Benedetto da Maiano, and is a work of exquisite decorative taste, in which the statues at the sides, leaning forward from their niches, augment the depth of the perspective vista in the central scene. By strict sculptural standards the ambivalent style of the relief represents a sad decline from the heights of the Cavalcanti Annunciation of Donatello, but it is impossible to repress a sense of pleasure at the delicate handling of the figures and at the subtlety with which the sculpture merges the interior architecture with the architecture of the frame" (*op.cit.*, p. 114). ¶ In preparation for carving the marble sculptures, Benedetto made a series of highly finished full-scale models in terracotta. Of these models three survive: a figure of St. John the Evangelist (Thyssen Collection, Madrid), and the two present sculptures, which represents God the father flanked by angels, and the angel of the annunciation, Gabriel. A version of the Madonna in terracotta may represent a fourth model, but its authenticity is still under discussion (Metropolitan Museum of Art, New York). ¶ The terracotta models are notably freer than the finished marbles. One crit-

Benedetto da Maiano, Altar of the Annunciation, S. Anna dei Lombardi, Naples

ic, Luitpold Dussler, has observed that the marbles display a "certain coldness . . . How different are the terracotta models. The angular ridged draperies of the clothes recede and one sees everywhere the evidence of the artist's hand in the sensitive modelling, the quiet feeling and the preference for broad surfaces and gradual modulations which avoid all hard edges" (*loc.cit.*, p. 21).

Attributed to ANTONIO RIZZO
(Verona c. 1440–1499/1500 Foligno)

7. *Saints Barbara and Agnes*

Marble, 81.9 x 43.2 cm. (32¼ x 17 inches), c. 1465

Antonio Rizzo was one of the leading figures in Venetian art at the end of the fifteenth century. As the Protomagister of the Palazzo Ducale after 1483, Rizzo helped to establish a new and more classical style in Venetian architecture and sculpture. His major projects included the *Scala dei Giganti* and the *Adam* and *Eve* for the Palazzo Ducale, and the Monument of Doge Nicolò Tron in the Frari. ¶ Previously unpublished, the present work bears a strong resemblance to various sculptures by Antonio Rizzo. The idealized, oval-shaped heads of the saints, with their large foreheads and pointed chins, resemble those of *Prudence* and *Charity* on the Tron tomb and are similar in form to that of *Eve*. The active and agitated drapery, with its angular folds, is especially like that of the angels on Rizzo's Altar of St. James (S. Marco, Venice). Moreover, the details of costume are similar. For example, on the underside of the angels' sleeves, the garment is buttoned at the center of the forearm, and forms two oval openings to either side of the button. The same detail is found in St. Barbara's sleeve. Finally, the cuffs of the saints' sleeves are identical in treatment to those of the Madonna in Antonio Rizzo's Altar of St. Clement (San Marco, Venice). ¶ The drapery of the present work bears a stronger resemblance to that of the angels on the Altar of St. James than to the freer and more elaborate drapery of the figures on the Tron Monument. Therefore, if the present work is indeed by Antonio Rizzo, it is likely to date from the early part of his career, perhaps circa 1465, the date inscribed on the Altar of St. Clement.

ANTONELLO GAGINI
(Palermo 1478–1536 Palermo)

8. *Resurrection of Christ*

Marble, 79 x 75 cm. (31 x 29½ inches), c. 1520–1530

For nearly 100 years beginning in the third-quarter of the fifteenth century, the Gagini family dominated the production of sculpture in Sicily and Southern Italy. They were artists of prodigious talent, especially Domenico, the patriarch of the family, who had been a pupil of Brunelleschi, and Antonello, who served as an assistant to Michelangelo, helping to carve the tomb of Pope Julius II. ¶ The present work can be confidently ascribed to Antonello Gagini; it is typical of his work, both in its details and overall conception. The soft languid folds of Christ's drapery, falling in long sinuous curves over his right leg resemble the drapery pattern found in many of his sculptures, for example, the statues of the *Madonna del Soccorso* (San Agostino, Sciacca) and *St. John the Evangelist* (Santa Maria Maggiore, Vibo Valentia). The rigid and angular rockery at the left is also characteristic of his style. It is highly similar to the forms of the rocks in the *Entombment*, one of the predella panels from the altarpiece of the Duomo of Palermo (dismantled; this panel is now in the Duomo of Nicosia). Furthermore, the poses of two of the soldiers are almost exactly like those of figures in other autograph works. The soldier seated in the left foreground should be compared with a figure in the right predella panel from the San Niccolò altar in Randazzo. On the other hand, the gesture of the soldier in the back at the right is very similar to that of one of the centurions in the *Conversion of Saul* on an altar in San Salvatore di Fitalia. Finally, the architectural details, such as the bases and capitals of the pilasters, and the simple moldings along the top and bottom of the main field, are exactly identical with those of two reliefs of the *Madonna and Child* by Antonello Gagini (Museo Civico, Termini Imerese and Galleria Nazionale, Palermo). ¶ Nearly all these parallels date from the 1520s: e.g., the Randazzo altarpiece was commissioned in 1522, the Palermo *Madonna and Child* in 1524, and the San Salvatore altarpiece in 1527. Therefore it is likely that the present work was also made during the 1520s. ¶ The Gagini specialized in the production of large scale altarpieces made up of interlocking relief panels and numerous standing figures. Possibly the present relief once formed part of such an altarpiece. However, as no other elements from that altarpiece appear to survive, its identity, location, size and patron cannot be established.

© 2001 Salander-O'Reilly Galleries, LLC
ISBN: 1-58821-089-8

Photography: Paul Waldman
Design: Lawrence Sunden, Inc.
Printing: Thorner Press